THE Bikini

Overleaf: Rolling down to Rio. Copperskinned Copacabana beach belles set the 1985 fashion of minimal bikinis turned down like tourniquets

THE Bikini

PRESENTED BY
PEDRO SILMON
WITH AN INTRODUCTION BY
MERIEL McCOOEY

DIADEM BOOKS

I would like to thank all the people whose help and encouragement made this book possible – colleagues on the Sunday Times Magazine, staff at Virgin Books, freelancers and friends.

I am particularly grateful to Meriel McCooey who very kindly agreed to write the introductory text, and to lend her name to the project. Special thanks go to Vincent Page for his advice and intrepid picture research which provided a wealth of visual material, from which I hope I have skimmed the cream. For the captions I am endebted to Rose Shepherd and Angela Wilkes whose patience and wit made the most of often very limited information and whose valiant subbing tied up many loose ends.

My sincere thanks to Richard Simon for securing the publishing contract with Virgin and for agreeing to represent such a small fish.

John Brown had the foresight and vision to agree to publish this book and to allow me to produce it in the way that it was originally conceived, with little compromise. Thanks are also due to Mike Allan, production manager, Jane Charteris, an immensely patient and understanding editor, and Dill Anstey who cleared all the picture permissions.

Lastly, my warmest thanks to my wife, Lesley, for her relentless enthusiasm and unfailing support.

Pedro Silmon, London, 1986

First published in 1986 by Virgin Books, 328 Kensal Road, London W10 5XJ

First published 1986 in the United States of America by Diadem Books

Distributed by Crown Publishers Inc., 225 Park Avenue South, New York, New York 10003

ISBN 0-517-61773-0

h g f e d c b a

Printed in Italy

CONTENTS

THE BIKINI STORY

BIKINI CHIC

BIKINI EXPOSURES

BIKINI MADNESS

BIKINI STARS

BIKINI PEOPLE

BIKINI GIRLS

THE BIKINI STORY

By Meriel McCooey

NO one man can be said to have 'invented' the bikini, for it is more emotion than notion, more gesture than garment. It is the smallest — the very smallest — concession that succeeding generations of sun-worshippers have been willing to make to modesty. It tests the limits of acceptability. It is a sop to society which says you can't go naked — and, teasingly, it contrives to be far more provocative than actual nudity ever could be.

As long ago as 1600 BC, Minoan wall paintings depicted the latest two-piece fashion. So Frenchman Louis Reard, an engineer by profession, was more than three-and-a-half millennia behind the times when he launched his version in 1946.

Still, they say there is nothing new under the sun (under the sun being where the bikini really comes into its own), and Reard, who died in 1984 at the age of 88, deserves to be remembered for bringing the bikini to popularity and for christening it.

On June 30 1946, the first post-war atom bomb test was carried out on Bikini Atoll in the South Pacific. Eighteen days later, Reard registered the name. The precise connection has never been established. When France Soir, a Parisian evening paper, invited its readers to hazard at Reard's reason for choosing 'Bikini', some larky

Pages 6 and 7: less than three weeks after the A-bomb test blasted Bikini Atoll in June 1946, Reard officially christened the bikini. His first model, Micheline (right), nude dancer from the Casino de Paris, was unabashed by the obvious tanning problems created by the sudden diminution

The newsy two-piece that fitted into a match-box, 1946. Others were slow to catch on; a year later singer Olga San Juan still wore armour-plating in Variety Girls

correspondent suggested that it was because it looked as if the wearer had just emerged from a bomb blast with a few shreds of clothing hanging from her – but how prettily arranged! More probably, Reard had in mind the 'bombshell' which he was about to drop on the civilised world, although he could not have anticipated the shock-waves that are felt in some corners of the globe even today (in Whitby, North Yorkshire, for example, it is still an offence to wear one).

Not that the first bikini was even so very different from the swimwear being worn ten or fifteen years before. In the early thirties, many a society lady sported a two-piece bathing-suit, though the lower half would have resembled shorts – a far cry from today's mini briefs, tangas and thongs. At this time, writer Cecily Hamilton recounted in her book, *Modern Germanies* (now, sadly, out of print), how she had observed a youngish woman walking on the beach of a lake near Berlin and wearing shorts or bathing drawers topped by a brassiere, an outfit that revealed a considerable expanse of bare midriff.

In 1938, designer Henry a la Pensee showed a beach suit of a short-sleeved, ankle-length coat over a bra and trunks in print material, to be worn with cork-soled, ankle-strap shoes. And from that same year, the Victoria and Albert Museum in London has a dazzling yellow, knitted woollen bra and pants beach ensemble which came from Finnegan's, a fashionable shop of the day in Bond Street.

By the end of the thirties, elasticated fabric was being used to make stretch swimsuits. Nylon, which was invented by the American firm, Du Pont, became available just before the War. Its drying properties, plus its gentle 'corset' effect, made it ideal material for bathing wear.

When Hollywood stars Ronald Reagan and Jane Wyman were photographed for Vogue in 1940 at Palm Springs, the then Mrs Reagan sported a Sharktex swimsuit, the shorts tight across the upper thigh, the halter-neck top snug-fitting, and between the two a good five inches of tanned skin.

Reard's bikini was simply smaller and more aggressively marketed than its predecessors. It started a gradual process of diminution which has reached its logical conclusion over recent years on the nudist beaches of Europe.

For many years, Reard ran a bikini shop in the Avenue de l'Opera in Paris. Splashed across the windows was the slogan, 'The original bikini is sold here'. It was, too, along with every other type, to suit every shape and in every colour. The shop's boast was that it sold over a hundred styles, including the first top to stay up without straps.

Louis Reard's suits could be packed into a matchbox printed with

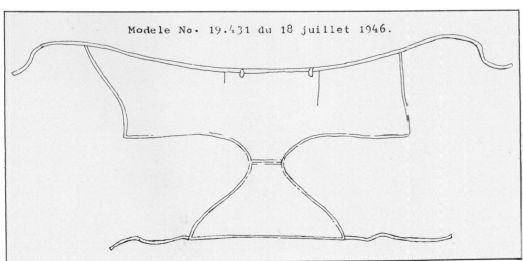

Modele No. 19.431 du 18 juillet 1946.

By the time mechanical engineer Louis Reard died at his home in Switzerland in 1984 at the age of 88, he'd been designing and marketing bikinis for almost forty years. His orginal design, dated 18 July 1946, was daringly cutaway

Cautious Middle America thought bikinis
'too much' until respectable stars
like Rita Hayworth posed in them, 1948

Miss Egypt, Marina Papaeliou, donned a
bikini to meet the Press at the 1953
Miss World contest. Although the organisers
had banned the garments from the
competition after 1951, they couldn't stop
contestants wearing them off-duty

a warning to those who might otherwise feel they'd been sold short that the two-piece comprised just thirty inches of cloth (a generous amount by some of today's standards).

Today, the shop sells sewing-machines.

It was the sensuous, pleasure-loving French who most wholeheartedly welcomed the bikini. Undoubtedly it represented, for them, a new spirit of freedom, an escape from the dismal, restrictive and austere years of the War.

"The suit is beginning to gather momentum," reported one voyeuristic Parisian newspaperman, "and finds favour with the naughty girls who decorate our sun-drenched beaches."

"Every year we arrived in Antibes," reminisces Diana Vreeland, empress of fashion, in her book, DV (Vintage Books, USA). "Everyone was water-skiing. Every girl was in a bikini. At the time I said the bikini was the biggest thing since the atom bomb, but I suppose bikinis started during the war — they probably just tore up bedsheets and made them."

The bikini was by no means so warmly received by all nations. The predominantly Roman Catholic Latin countries found the new swimwear unacceptable. In 1951, the first Miss World contest was staged to publicise the Festival of Britain. Bikinis were de rigueur for contestants. But, although they were by now the height of fashion, the tiny two-pieces were an affront to many countries' sensibilities. In the second contest, the bikini was scrapped in favour of a one-piece costume, and has been banned by the organisers ever since.

Surprisingly, since they are usually so passionate about clothes

Glamour, British vintage 1955, was Diana Dors teetering on a gondola in an over-the-top £150 mink creation at the Venice Film Festival. Gallic sex kitten Brigitte Bardot needed nothing more than dangling straps to make her sultry point, filming at St Tropez, 1961. Buoyant American movie queen Jayne Mansfield required hundreds of identical extras for this take for Life magazine, 1957

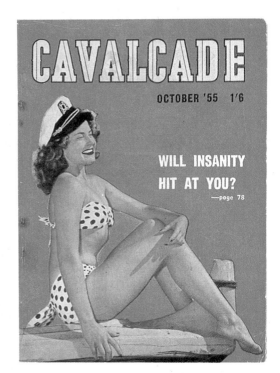

Bikini-clad girls added a certain allure to popular journals and, it was hoped, sold more copies, Australia 1955

Opposite above: the Copenhagen fashion-conscious were promised that this was "something of the naughtiest seen yet for the beach – zip-zip," 1966

Opposite below: womanly figures and any pretence at practicality were long gone with the wind after the introduction of teasing lace tangas, France 1975

and looking fashionable, even American women didn't really take to the bikini when it first appeared. Californians, who spend so much of their time draped around pools, thought them 'too much' (meaning, of course, too little). And straight-laced, puritanical Middle America utterly condemned the new suits as being fast, flash and louche.

It was not until the more graceful stars, such as the sensational Rita Hayworth, Paulette Goddard, that luscious sexpot Terri Moore, and eventually the absolutely unignorable Marilyn Monroe, chose to be photographed in versions of the bikini that American womanhood finally accepted it as normal beachwear.

By modern standards, not all stars and starlets were so tasteful an advertisement for Reard's creation. Diana Dors, in a little mink number, and the well-endowed Jayne Mansfield were not the sort of images on which today's women model themselves.

But all through the fifties, the ultra-feminine form was in vogue, and a well-defined and generous bustline was much admired. Bikini tops were boned or wired for maximum uplift, and even padded to make the most of the smaller bosom. (This was the decade, after all, when advertisers in America dreamed up 'training bras' for little girls, fostering the belief that these improbable garments would encourage the breasts to develop).

In 1954 one Simone Silva had her bikini top removed by Robert Mitchum in the sea during the Cannes Film Festival. The spectacle caused a furore (three photographers fell into the water, two sustaining broken bones, in the scramble to get a closer look), but the publicity stunt brought Ms Silva no lasting fame.

Now that Hollywood was overcoming its initial resistance to the fashion, a new genre of moving pictures was born. American International Pictures brought to the screen such cinematic nonsenses as Bikini Beach and How to Stuff a Wild Bikini (first catch your bikini?). Even sillier, perhaps, was the 1960 hit song about the girl who didn't dare to bare as much as she thought she would in her "itsy-bitsy, teeny-weeny, yellow polka-dot bikini".

Silver screen starlets began to go further than mere publicity poses, actually wearing two-pieces in their films. In 1956 Brigitte Bardot starred in Roger Vadim's And God Created Woman, in which she appeared in the briefest of bikinis and with the sexiest of pouts, establishing herself for ever in our minds as the French sex kitten. Two years later the first Carry On film was released in Britain. Since then we have grown used to the sight of the voluptuous Barbara Windsor in a variety of bikinis – Miss Windsor figuring very large, the bikini figuring very small indeed.

But perhaps the most sensational bikini-clad body ever to stride out of the water was that of Ursula Andress in the 1963 James Bond film, Dr No. That image of the tall and beautiful Swiss actress, knife tucked in bikini and a maquillage of plain sea-water, became a symbol of sensuality around the world.

Not all starlets, however, were prepared to reveal so much of themselves. Esther Williams, the acquatic actress whom Samuel Goldwyn recognised as 'a star when wet', never wore a bikini: as a former champion she took even her cinematic swimming seriously.

By 1964 a curious and even more revealing item of beachwear hit the headlines. It was the creation of American designer Rudi Gernreich and consisted of bikini pants held up by braces.

Model Peggy Moffat was photographed in this topless garment. The Daily Mirror challenged its readers, "Would you wear it?" The French dismissed it as a gimmick and banned it. "Elle rejects this," said that august magazine at the time: "not fashion, not an idea but a joke." But the edition of Woman's Wear Daily that featured it on the cover swiftly sold out, and even the editor's copy was stolen from his office.

American store buyers had few reservations about Gernreich's suit. Reputable stores like Nieman Marcus, Henri Bendel and Bonwit Teller ordered them by the hundred. Beauty queen Beverley Isherwood wore one made from £20,000 worth of platinum. She never got it wet and, after she had modelled it in a Manchester store, it was sent off to be melted down.

The bikini, however, was not eclipsed and continued to make news. In North Wales, for instance, a building-site foreman working next to the municipal baths ordered a screen to be erected to prevent the bikini-clad bathers from distracting his workmen. "The costumes leave little to the imagination," he complained. "What red-blooded male could turn his back on such a scene?"

A Nottingham nightclub owner offered cut-price entrance to girls who turned up wearing bikinis. He was accused of sexual discrimination, so he made the same offer to men.

A model in the Midlands, Diane Lowe, showed off a most sensational suit made from shrimp nets and called the 'sea-through' suit.

Two rival pull-ups for lorry and car drivers near York went into fierce competition. Both cafés were run by women, and one trumped the other when she took to wearing a bikini to serve her appreciative customers. Business, not surprisingly, boomed.

The sixties saw the advent of the crochet bikini, and of a version with a low, belted waist that mimicked the hipster look then in fashion. In the latter part of the decade, Bardot and her pouting followers took to sunbathing topless, and did more than anyone to put St Tropez on the map. The bikini, at its briefest yet, was everywhere worn with two vital accessories: a golden tan and a mane of long hair.

Today's designers are constantly seeking to modernise the bikini: Liza Bruce brings a tougher and more independent look to the beach in 1985

Pages 18 and 19: sunworship in Brazil, where the girls still go for a thong in exotic jungle prints, 1985

Psychologist Jon Collen believes that the choice of one's bikini can reveal as much about mind as body. Those who choose the thong, he said in an article in the Sunday Telegraph Magazine, expose the three main areas of male attraction (breasts, bottom and legs) in an attempt to disguise their shyness, to draw attention away from the face. Such women lack confidence in anything but their bodies. The regular bikini is the choice of the truly confident woman: the costume covers what has to be covered, but reveals a modest amount without shocking. The mini bikini, on the other hand, is a desperate cry for attention. The woman who wears it is looking for superficial relationships so she flaunts her sexuality aggressively.

Certainly, imperfections of a merely physical nature — lumpy thighs, overflowing busts, thickening waists and flabby stomachs — have never inhibited women from donning miniscule scraps of gaudy material the better to enjoy the sun. To look its best, the bikini calls for perfectly smooth, taut skin without a square inch of superfluous flesh obtruding any where.

Swimwear has long been influenced by trends in the general fashion of the day — as well as by mores and morals, and psychological and physical considerations. The bikini is no exception: it has been trimmed with frills, sequins, diamanté, suede, net and even shells. Around the mid-seventies, the briefs became very brief indeed. Enter the string, the thong (which was banned in Cannes as recently as 1980), the theatrical G-string, the rikini, the loop and something known as the 'Savage', which was actually no more than two Vs of fabric tied at the sides and joined under the crotch. (Around this time, dedicated wearers of every new style must have noticed that the price of bikinis increased in inverse proportion to the amount of material used!)

Having been reduced to a bare minimum, the bikini is now appearing in what might be called 'multi-choice' forms. British firm Trulo makes a Lycra suit called the Expose, which starts off as a prim cover-all but rolls down into a monokini. Trulo also makes the Che Kee, an ensemble of brief bra top and boxer shorts that roll into a G-string.

One of the very latest ideas originated in Rio, where the beaches stretch for miles, as do the bronzed and lithe-limbed girls. This suit consists of skimpier than skimpy bra top and comparatively substantial pants. The trick is to roll the pants down until they just cover the private parts. The minimal top may be discarded altogether. Underwear queen Janet Reger was so impressed by what she saw on a trip to Rio that she designed her own range based on the Brazilian costumes.

The bikini continues to fascinate the cream of the fashion world, who are forever playing around with the basic two-piece. Brilliant

American designer Norma Kamali started making suits, which she describes as "sassy, on the cute side of sexy", in 1980. It was she who introduced the wet look that almost every other manufacturer has emulated.

Then there's Liza Bruce, who puts holes where holes oughtn't to be, and who makes Day-glo look positively delicate. And Kathy Methven, who designs over-the-top, exotic and fantastic suits, in suede and hung to death with beads, real show-stoppers that cost the earth.

The recent emphasis on health and fitness has also had an effect on swimwear. The trend towards the stronger, better-muscled female form is being reflected on the beach as it is on the street. The bikini was never practical for swimming, or any other energetic pursuit, and the growth in popularity of such physically hard exercises as weight-lifting and aerobics has taken its toll: over the past two or three years, one-piece bathing-suits have outsold two-pieces and have taken on a decidedly sporty aspect. Even the very functional maillot of the thirties has made a comeback. (Professional body-builders, however, still prefer the bikini to show off their muscles to best advantage.)

But the one-piece costume is perhaps not so much of a threat to the bikini as is the trend towards nudity. The fact that summer boutiques everywhere are selling bikini bottoms alone is proof that topless sunbathing is not just a passing fad. We are more than halfway to accepting naked bathing as the norm.

There is nothing new of course about nude bathing. The ancient Greeks and Romans would have been very puzzled by the habit of donning clothes only to get them wet. In the matter of dress, a topless look was favoured by the Cretan-Minoans, while the dernier cri in Roman leisurewear was a garment bearing a striking resemblance to the two-piece designed by Louis Reard.

Historically, the bikini came into being just as post-war holiday-makers were rediscovering the delights of sun-drenched beaches and as many more were tasting them for the first time. As the travel industry has thrived, so has the beachwear business, and in particular the bikini. It is simply a reaction to the sun. It allows us to expose to those beneficent rays just as much as is prudent or decent. And as standards of decency change, so we dare to bare ever more. Since the anything-goes days of the sixties, anything — and sometimes everything — has gone.

But the bikini is not about to disappear altogether. The fashion industry, ever inventive, will always rise to the challenge of creating some irresistible little number to win over the naturists and narcissists. And, as always, the bikini will be favoured as more erotic, even, than skin.

Proud to be pregnant: a Mediterranean wader appreciates her freedom from the constrictions of the clinging one-piece

BIKINI CHIC

THE bikini is born — and straightway almost disappears. Within two short years of its arrival, Louis Reard's revealing creation had been, as it were, bowdlerised, and in 1948 even he was designing costumes that were not much more (or less) than pretty beach editions of brassières and knickers. These were whittled down through the fifties and sixties. By the end of the seventies, tops barely covered nipples, pants were cut narrow at the front and back, high at the sides. The Body Beautiful generation truly found itself in the eighties: tops were discarded altogether, pants turned into G-strings and thongs. It took at least thirty years to catch up with Reard, even longer to go beyond.

Top: Reard bikinis 1948. After the initial revelations, decorum reasserted itself in the bra-and-pantie-girdle style that ruled for a staid decade (right, 1950)

Left: Klein of Montreal's Festival of Britain bikini, with Big Ben and South Bank fireworks, was only slightly more revealing than his dark gold, strapless swimsuit, 1951

Post-rationing extravagance: a gold bikini comes with a sharkskin, kid-trimmed jacket during a fashion show at London store, Marshall and Snelgrove, 1953

The cover-all jacket is still in evidence but the pants are trimmer in this ensemble shown during a display of Commonwealth and UK fashions, all made of Lancashire cotton, at the Café Royale, 1957

Right: coals to Newcastle? British fashion goes on a ten-day luxury yacht cruise along the Cote d'Azur in 1955, sponsored by Picture Post, to show itself off

High Fashion steps in when Norman Parkinson takes Pastrie, one of his favourite models, to Tahiti to pose in a Jaeger chiffon bikini, 1960

Right: less exotic, if curious, locations were used for High Street fashion. Although the jacket has gone, a wrap-around skirt is provided in the name of modesty with this op-art suit from Caprice, 1966

Overleaf: by the turn of the decade designers were daring more. Carefully placed peekaboo cutouts and holes sustained interest in these 1971 French bikinis from Britt Marie Nystroen (left) and Nautic of Paris

A well-sited flower counters possible embarrassment — and adds a touch of naughtiness — for the wearer of this Britt Marie Nystroen crochet suit, 1969

Top sixties model Paulene Stone sports a topically mind-bending floral print bikini (still underwired) and the fashionable, ironed-straight fringe, 1967

Model Vilma poses winningly in a bright red, gladiator-style bikini in wet-look fabric from design-house Celon, 1970

His 'n' Hers: beachwear reflects the advent of the 'unisex' look with 'Frederick' (his) and 'Tiger Eye' (hers) in four-colour print material, from the Tweka collection for 1972

Opposite: for those flatter than diving-boards only, this American design has nothing in the way of support, but the by-now popular back-tying halter added a measure of safety, 1977

Left: Mark Bohan's flattering halter-necked bra and sarong-style bottom used lots of fabric and cost a bomb. The haute couture bikini, Dior, early seventies

Opposite: rounder,
fitter figures of the
mid-seventies
were shown to best
advantage by
simple, uncluttered
lines, exemplified
by Christine Bailly's
suit for Olympic, 1976

Realism enters
fashion photography
in the form of
freckles and water
droplets in this shot
for Elle magazine of
Olympic's snazzy
1975 style

Above: nautical but nice, Italian design as featured in Annabella magazine, 1978

Right: practical American designers supplied a polythene hip-bag for all those beach essentials — suntan lotion, lip salve and, for the health-conscious, an apple, 1977

Enter the monokini. It needed the deepest of tans, careful attention with the razor and, naturally, a perfect bosom, 1979

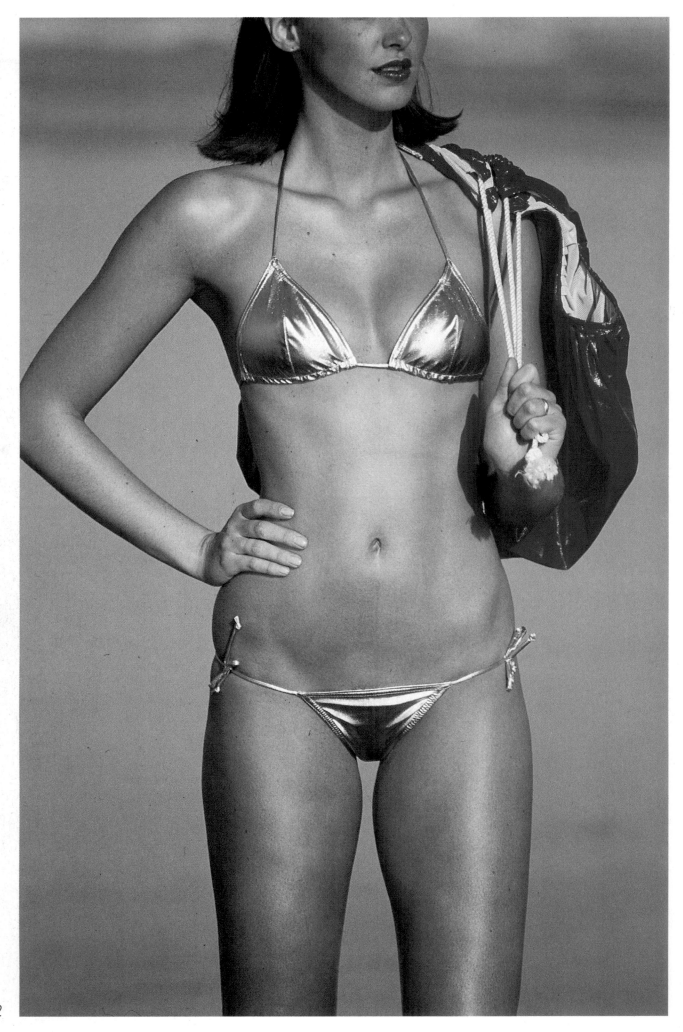

PVC ensemble from Biba may have looked cool, but despite diminished proportions it made sunbathers melt, France, 1982

Right: athletic Italian design harks back to earlier times — better, perhaps, for serious swimmers, but something of a flop with modern beach youth, 1984

Sabu-turbanned
Countess Pilar Crespi,
a Norman Parkinson
favourite, cools
down orphan
elephants at a Sri
Lankan sanctuary,
in a Norma Kamali
bikini, 1980

Left: dog-walking on the promenade becomes eye-catching exercise in a Fiorucci bikini set off by an evening shirt and giant sparkler, Elle, 1983

Right: with bras no longer obligatory a vibrant acrylic sweater tops a virtual G-string for those off-beach strolls, from Nulle Part Ailleurs, 1984

Overleaf: laid-back Latin Americans sweat it out in the latest fashion — 'multi-choice' suits that roll up or down to cover as much or as little as you like

BIKINI EXPOSURES

THE *paparazzi, that enterprising, if ill-bred bunch of photographers who chase celebrities round the world, owe almost as much to Louis Reard as they do to the inventor of the zoom lens, the sine qua non of their profession. Illicit, grainy long-shots of female celebrities in bikinis offer a greedily grateful public hitherto unimagined intimacy with the rich and famous, secrets previously well hidden by expensive clothes becoming common knowledge. Not surprisingly, some of those intruded upon seek redress in the courts. But it's a photographer's maxim that if you're royal, rich and famous, or any one of them, you're public property, especially if you're wearing a bikini.*

*Top: German actress Elke Sommer hides from prying eyes at Alicante,
early seventies. Right: a drooling Princess Stephanie of Monaco is caught in the act of adjusting her bikini*

Left: Princess Stephanie wet-bikes in the South of France with Anthony Delon, son of Alain, 1984

Above: the Duke and Duchess of Kent not beyond public scrutiny on a private holiday, Corfu, 1983

Princess Caroline's smile as she takes her daughter for a stroll shows that sneaky photography doesn't have to be a humiliating revelation, 1984

Family secrets: Christina Onassis (right) reveals nothing more than a healthy appetite and light mood on an anniversary holiday on the family island of Scorpios, 1979. Step-mother Jackie (far right), putting herself through the pinch-flab test, is blissfully unaware of the photographer zooming in, 1972

56

Ever the star, actress
Joan Collins, with
daughter Tara
on the Italian Riviera,
awaits the arrival of
then-spouse
Anthony Newley
and turns a
snatched picture to
her advantage, 1964

Strolling along her private St Tropez beach with some dogged admirers in 1984, Brigitte Bardot looks every bit a good as she had on the set

of The Contempt, Capri 1963. She and the bikini were made for each other

Stars in focus: Marilyn Monroe (above), more off-balance than off-guard, 1955;
Jayne Mansfield (below) with her family, Villefranche, 1962; Jane Fonda (right)
in pre-workout days, enjoying a binge during filming in the South of France, 1964

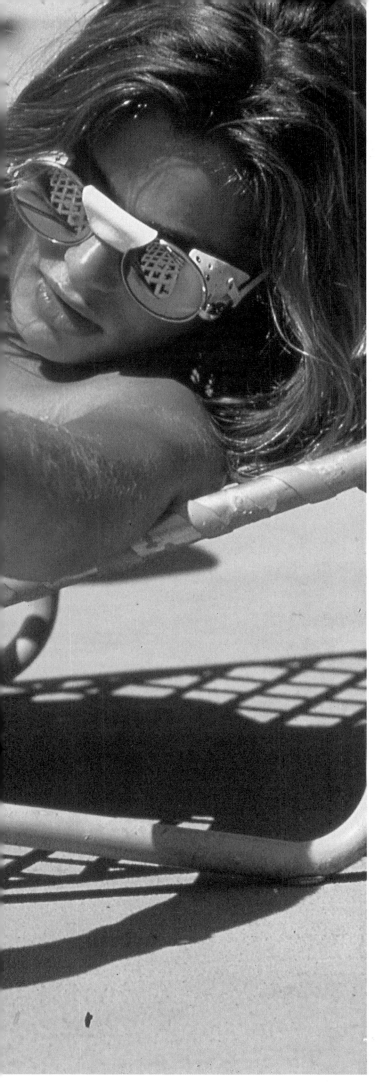

Black on black:
angular singer
Grace Jones makes
no concessions to
her name,
although bikini and
Caribbean turban
are stylishly
elegant, 1982

Nastassja Kinski
takes time out after
the success of Tess
to feed a squirrel
and gives someone
a tasty snapshot
in the process,
Hollywood, 1980

BIKINI
MADNESS

SINCE its inception the bikini has attracted certain eccentric designers and wild fantasists. Female anatomy has been the subject of jokes for centuries, and the bikini, which effortlessly draws attention to the areas most frequently lampooned, presents irresistible opportunites for visual puns. Some are genuinely witty, others merely daft, most utterly impractical. Desperate news editors with a blank space to fill have often been thankful for pictures of pretty girls in 'cat' or 'butterfly' suits, usually accompanied by a 'cor, look at that' caption. Even so, such silly and preposterous notions must offer a cheerier prospect over the breakfast table than indiscriminate nudity.

Top: it was a courageous girl who risked the suntan patterns created by this piece
of zaniness, 1967. Right: summer in the city, and onlookers, not unnaturally, can't quite believe their eyes

Left: an expensive boob? Constanze, Parisian silversmith, toiled 100 hours to make her Amazonian outfit, which cost around £3,000 in 1980

Right: Denise Wixey models the leonine knockers that she designed, April 1975

It would be hard to beat for bad taste American Arthur Essency's diabolical design, inspired, he said, by the feeling that 1975's swimwear was too modest

69

70   *Marlene Selden, dabbler in "weird and wonderful inventions," designed these to give a cool personal breeze and ward off intrusive flies.*

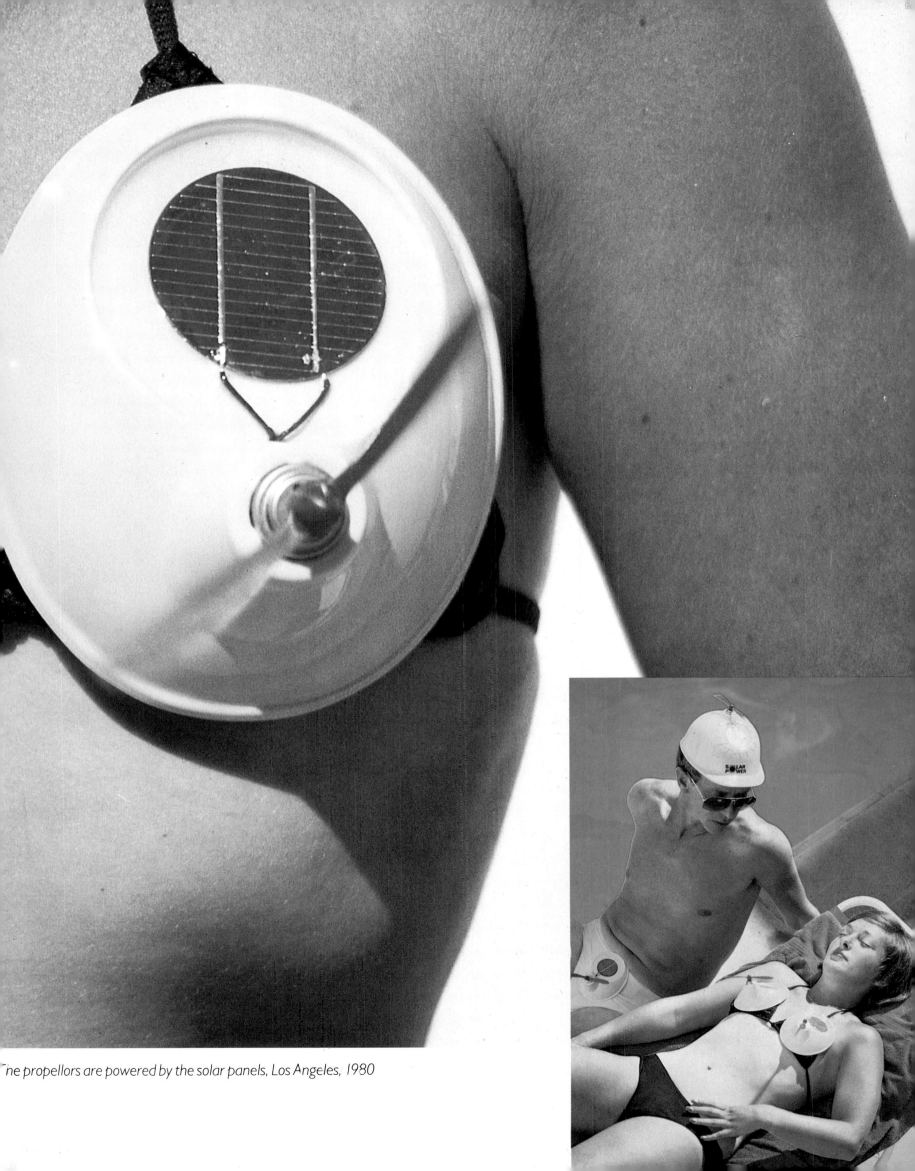

The propellors are powered by the solar panels, Los Angeles, 1980

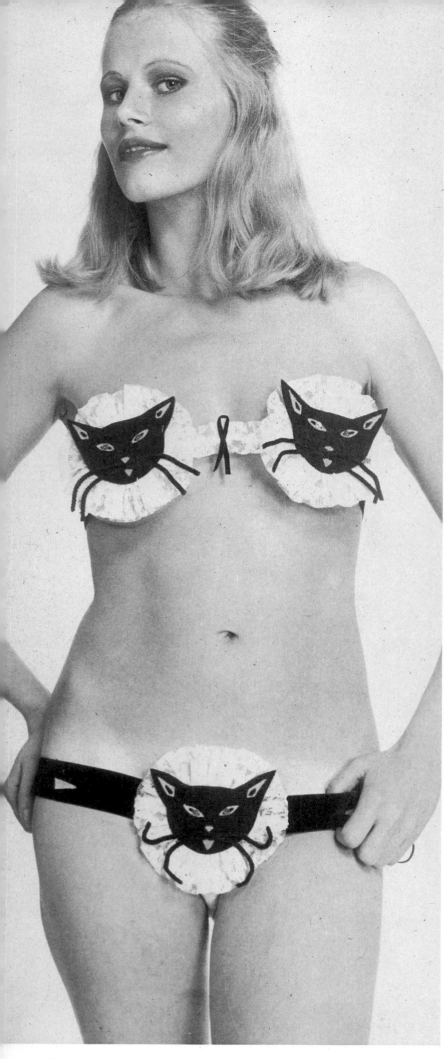

72   *Self-expression or male fantasy? European designs dating from the late sixties and early seventies*

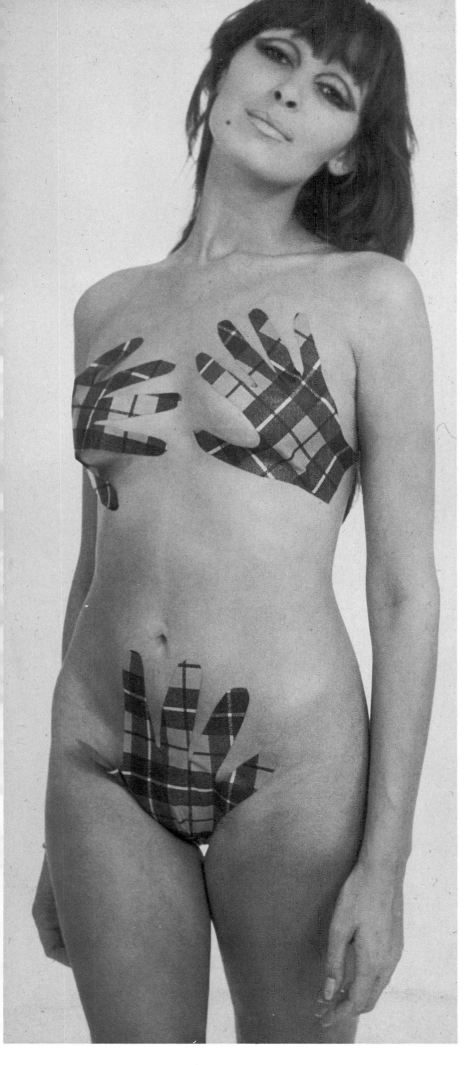

Witty window dressing adds a surreal new chapter to the bikini storey. Springs Building, New York, 1985

Right: stealing the shirt off your man's back, 1966, an idea by Nicholas Hoogstraten

Above: 1968 Olympia Boat Show, London. Below: 1971 Earl's Court Motor Show, London. Don't car radios always get pinched?

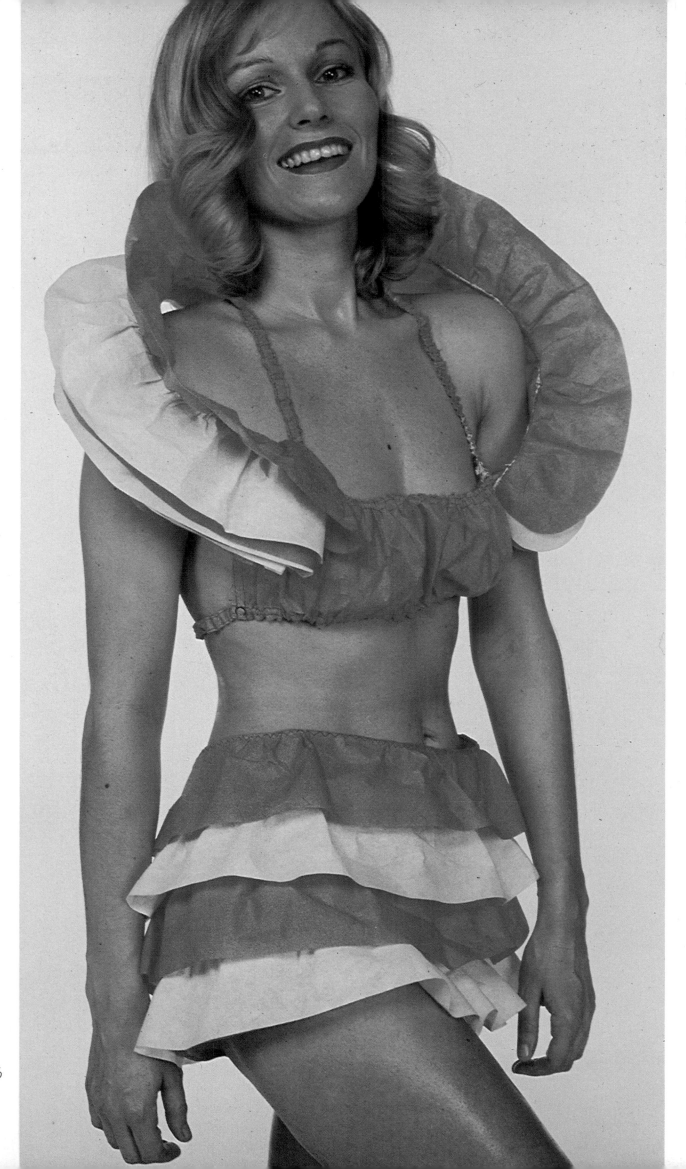

Left: Paco Rabanne's 1973 crêpe paper bikini, more suited to a carnival than the beach

Right: it's 1976 and punk produces a suitably impractical version in dimpled leather and chains

A prickly pair from Paris: Luc Traineau's 1966
made-to-measure real hair bikini (above) was washable.
Berns' 1965 hedgehog skins were, one hopes, washed

Above: model Susan Sinclair tucks into the latest diet — edible bikinis. This one had liquorice straps with bra and pants in passion fruit or cherry flavours

Left: if you can't afford real silver, follow Tina Hunt's example. She decorated her bikini with foil milk-bottle tops to get that extra touch of individuality, 1967

Right: the top two-thirds of this tricky trikini, designed by Leone Paule of Sydney, had to be literally glued on — and removed with methylated spirits

Something
BLOOD CURDLING
for Everyone!

...when a pretty GHOUL
trades in her bed sheet
for a BIKINI!

AMERICAN INTERNATIONAL'S
GHOST IN THE INVISIBLE BIKINI
in PATHÉCOLOR AND PANAVISION

STARRING TOMMY KIRK · DEBORAH WALLEY · ARON KINCAID · HARVEY LEMBECK · JESSE WHITE · CLAUDIA MARTIN
NANCY SINATRA WITH GUEST STAR BASIL RATHBONE and PATSY KELLY
SUSAN HART AS THE GHOST   BORIS KARLOFF AS HIRAM STOKELY

BIKINI STARS

BEAUTIFUL *faces, firm flesh, perfect figures: what could be more natural accompaniments to the bikini? From the first, rising starlets and some stars eagerly exploited the combination in studio publicity shots and, gradually, in films. The effect was electric. Never mind that most of them would have had just as much poise, allure and sex-appeal in bin-liners; bikini-clad, they shone like beacons. Rita Hayworth smouldered from posters, Ursula Andress rose majestic from the waves in Dr No, Brigitte Bardot barely needed to act. Although the glamorous partnership between stars and the bikini has had its heyday, Bond adventures will no doubt continue to give them equal billing.*

Attempts to make the bikini beastly for horrific B-movies (top) were doomed. Better to hang one on a shapely beauty such as the young Brigitte Bardot (right) as The Lighthouse Keeper's Daughter, 1952

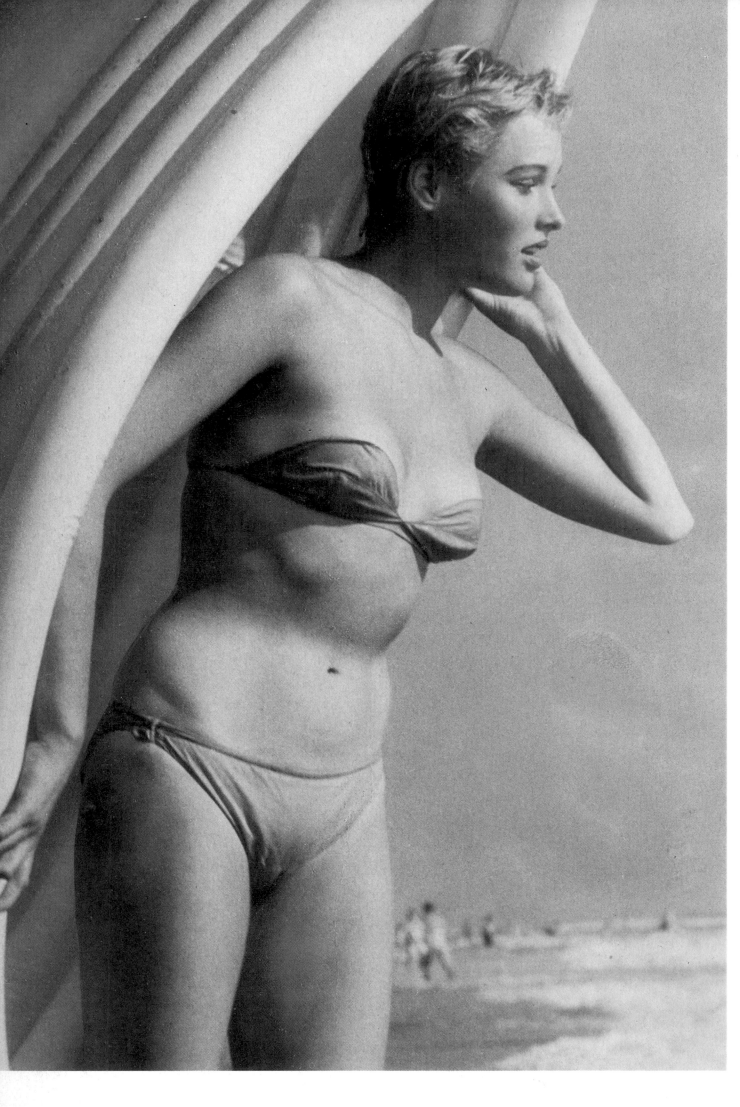

Swiss screen
goddess Ursula
Andress looked just
as terrific (right)
when she rose
Venus-like from the
waves in the Bond
adventure, Dr No,
in 1963, as she had
at 18 (left), carrying
her rubber boat on
Ostia Beach, Italy,
1954

Above: Sophia Loren's bikini may be bulky, her figure in those days fuller, but winning bathing belle contests like this shot her to fame

Right: A centrestage Diana Dors shines out from other young luminaries on this stairway of British starlets in Lady Godiva Rides Again, 1951

American actress Mamie Van Doren (opposite), 1960, and Britain's Joan Collins, circa 1955, in publicity shots of contrived exoticism   87

88   Ann Dvorak, in 'natural' promotional still

Linda Cristal, Hollywood's first Argentine star, showing the extent of her tan

US servicemen's favourite pump-girl, Ava Gardner, was, said MGM, "a strong swimmer" 89

1948: bikinis have definitely arrived, worn (above) by Southern California starlets shortlisted for Irving Berlin's film Easter Parade, and (right) by dancer Cyd Charisse who needed no cutaway sides to emphasise her famous, endless legs

British actress, Susan Hampshire, circa 1960

Shipmate Carolyn Jones, Sail a Crooked Ship, 1961

One-time Lyons Corner House nippy, Joan Rice, 1950

Left: American 'peaches and cream,' Virginia Mayo, 1952

Sultry Italian star Maria Canale, 1958

Above: starlet Nadia Roc says bonjour to a couple of sailors at the 1964 Cannes Film Festival

Left: actor George Baker and two leading ladies romp in pursuit of publicity at the 1956 festival

In some films bikinis seemed to have little to do with beaches and a lot to do with sex. Above: the film that introduced Tammy the Wonder Tarantula to the subject. Right: Russ Meyer's favourite leading lady, Kitten Natividad, needed no such introduction, 1976

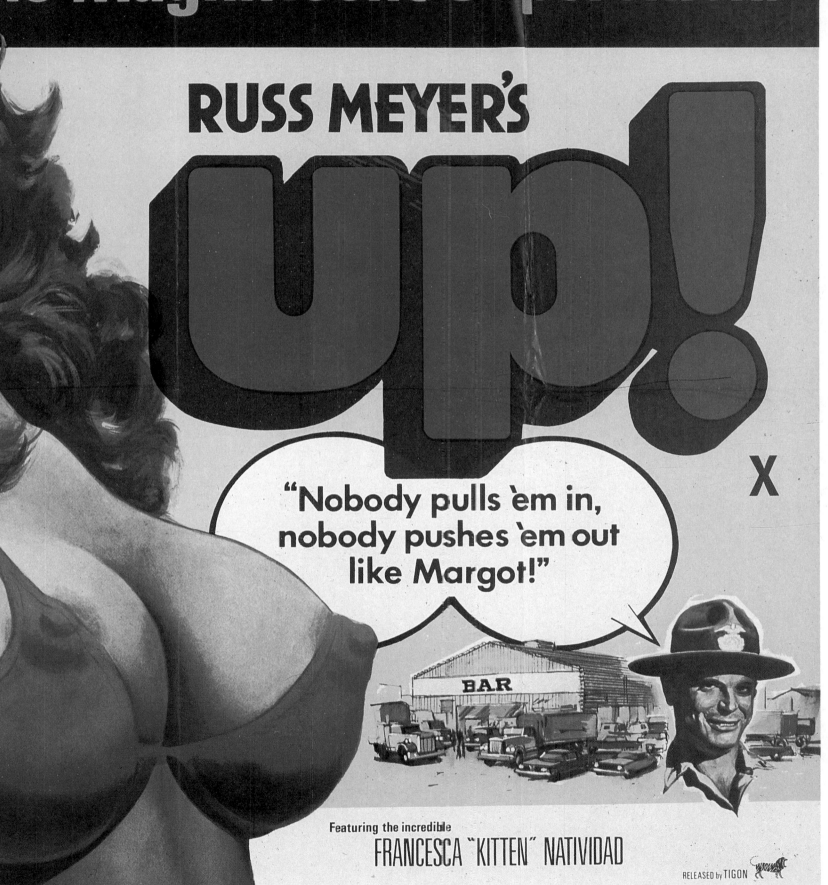

Jayne Mansfield,
borne aloft by her
Tarzan, boyfriend
Mickey Hartigay,
shows how a wild
bikini really ought
to be stuffed.
At the Publicists'
Association
Ballyhoo Ball,
Hollywood, 1956

The increasingly
buxom blonde, who
probably came
closer than anyone
since Mae West to
fulfilling America's
pneumatic ideals,
could still adopt a
fetching pose
(right) in 1963. But
by 1966 (overleaf),
a year before her
death, her
phenomenal form
was more than
a mere bikini
was ever meant to
contain

104   *Marilyn Monroe began with a good-time-girl image, circa 1950 (page 102), but quickly developed that famous, lip-parted come-hither look,*

1951 (page 103), and appealing vulnerability. Above right, in Clash by Night, 1952

Raquel Welch
always had her
bikinis tailor-made
to do justice to her
splendid hour-glass
figure. Left: in The
Biggest Bundle of
Them All, 1966.
Above: on location
in Miami, 1968

A starry array of blondes in bikinis — the North European ideal? Above: German expressionism with Elke Sommer looking deadlier than the male. Below: gun-toting Swede Britt Ekland in Bondage, The Man with the Golden Gun, 1974. Right: Julie Christie, a British Darling, 1965. Far right: Norwegian Julie Ege, of whom every home should have one

BIKINI
PEOPLE

FROM Barbados to the Black Sea, on beaches the world over the bikini really comes into its own. Ripening teenagers and mature young women present as glamorous an image as the stars did, but their plumper and older sisters manifest quite different dimensions. Sand and sea are dispensable, however; sun is the one prerequisite for the bikini-wearer. And in the certain knowledge that wherever it shines, be it on beach, poolside, London street or Leningrad wall, bikini-wearers will find a way, swimwear manufacturers produce the garments in many sizes in accommodatingly stretchy fabric Sun-worship renders all equal, but, as ever, some remain more (or less) equal than others.

Real people, unlike models or film stars, tend to cram a lot more flesh into their two-pieces than Monsieur Reard might ever have intended. Sun-seekers at resorts on the Black Sea (above) and the Brazilian coast (right)

*A California belle (above) lives out the
eternal triangle — runner, stick and dog, 1970*

*Beach play: the Royal Airforce joins in local
activities (left) at Vallone, Italy, 1982*

118   *Supine Soviet in not-so teenie-weenie polka dots, Black Sea*

Left: a far-sighted and provocative promenader rings the changes from Kiss Me Quick hats, 1969. Right: a handy pair of twentieth-century breastplates, 1974. Opposite: sturdy-thighed roller-skater rehearses for Newcastle to London charity pram push, 1971

"I hear she married a Second Lieutenant. The first one got away."

"I THOUGHT IT WAS A MISERABLE LITTLE THING!"

I HOPE TO GO AROUND IN EVEN LESS TOMORROW JOHN'

"THIS REMINDS ME, JACK IS DATING ME TO-NIGHT"

122   *The girls, like the humour, were overblown on seaside postcards and the bikinis usually the prerogative of the youthful sexpot, not the large,*

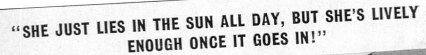

"SHE JUST LIES IN THE SUN ALL DAY, BUT SHE'S LIVELY ENOUGH ONCE IT GOES IN!"

"HE'S AN OFFICER IN ONE OF THOSE AFRICAN REGIMENTS—HIS PRIVATES ARE ALL BLACK OF COURSE..."

"I HAD A WEEKEND IN PARIS — AND THEY WERE NO BETTER THAN OURS!"

12093 She:—"Of course, you can stay in as long as you like, so long as you come out before dinnertime!"

"I hear you've got a groom at last." "Yes, I had to work like a horse to get him."

irate wife. Vulgar, perennial and peculiarly British, they are still sent in their thousands

Holiday camps became ever more popular in post-war Britain, and one of the main attractions was the beauty contest, Cook's camp, Prestatyn, Wales, 1947

Right: campers snapped relaxing outside their chalets by Picture Post, which did many a survey on the new leisure centres, Filey, North Yorkshire, 1953

Florida girls line up for a bikini contest at a free concert by Beach Boy Mike Love during the Easter college vacation, 1983

A brave No. 52 sports a prototype bikini in a Butlins holiday camp beauty contest, Filey, North Yorkshire, 1946

A Russian belle on holiday is doubly appreciated, Sochi, Black Sea, 1961

After a long, hard winter, Leningradians prop up the wall of the Peter and Paul Fortress to soak in the spring's first weak sunshine in an overall noonday temperature of as little as 10°C below zero, March 1983

BIKINI GIRLS

WEARING a bikini for some is almost a profession. Models are often required to parade in them to promote all manner of unrelated products, from racing cars to magazines. And all because the girl-in-the-bikini, more symbolic than sexual, could apparently sell an abbatoir to a vegetarian. Other professionals wear them in the name of a little self-promotion, such as Miss Worlds, or the bodybuilders whose cultivated musculature, considered by many to be unfeminine, is shown to best advantage by a scanty two-piece. With the recent rise in popularity of the one-piece suit among beach belles, perhaps it is up to these working girls to carry on Louis Reard's tradition.

Top: incongruous pairing in the name of sales at the 1971 Olympia Motor Racing Car Show, London.
Right: fifties version of the same soft-sell approach on a sun lounger guaranteed to leave a lasting impression

134   *Even when promoting beach equipment, models were often confined to a studio, Cape Town*

Budding ballerina Carol Jean Lauritzer lists among her hobbies "eating spaghetti with pizza as a side dish," Florida, 1957

Right: a primmer
pin-up inspires
dreams of far-off
places

Joan Faya Bennett,
scissor-legs happily in
the Sarasota surf
to make a cheerful
splash for pin-up
collectors

Overleaf: a hand-
held German
calendar shot of
exotic sensuality,
1970

Nordic blondes or tropical brunettes, calendars have a different girl for every month: left, pouting and pasty-lipped Bardot imitator, 1970, and opposite, a titillating model from 1981

*Form and content:
Travel and Leisure
magazine shot for
the 'quiet of the
Bahamas,' 1982*

*Fifteen feet under
the Red Sea a girl
with lead weights in
her wellingtons adds
sought-after colour
to a book on
underwater
photography, 1981*

Opposite: actress
Mary Margaret
Hume personifies
the natural and
healthy look that has
become the vogue
for bikini girls, 1981

Right: the Bahamas
entice again with
the promise of
palm-fringed frolics
in a balmy paradise,
1975

Overleaf: Paulina,
in a chamois bikini
from Sunset Beach
by Catalina, is
serenaded on a
didgeridoo by
aborigines, at The
Pinnacles, West
Australia, 1985

Body language
speaks volumes for
the hard sell: the
Ford Skylite
Accessory Sun Roof,
1985 (above), and
(right) a Heaven's
Angel on the Sigma
stand, Earl's Court
Motor Cycle Show,
London, 1980,
courtesy of the
famous Bardot
biker poster

Overleaf: hidden
persuaders fiddle
with their focusing
on the back of
this imaginatively
laid-out 1963
magazine
cover/advert

148

ILFORD colour films
give brilliant results in any camera

WHAT'S MORE, THEY COST LESS!

To take your finest-ever holiday pictures choose from: Ilfochrome 32—for superb colour transparencies; Ilfocolor — for wonderful colour prints.

You'll find fuller details of both these films in full-page colour advertisements inside this issue. Buy them from any chemist or photographic dealer—use them in any camera of any make!

150

TODAY'S LEADER IN COLOUR **ILFORD** naturally!

EVERY TUESDAY   Week ending April 13, 1963

TODAY
6^D   The New JOHN BULL

BINGO!
£100
AND IT'S FREE!

MY MAN WAS THE
STRIP CLUB KILLER
by BETTE MELVIN   page 6

KENNETH
MORE
GOES... **X**   page 16

£80,000 LAND RUSH
page 3   —why champagne is
flowing in the Lea Valley

OH, CHÉRIE—AND SHE'S   page 8
WAITING TO BE KISSED!

ALL THE COLOUR
PICTURES IN THIS   Special
feature
page 19
ISSUE WERE TAKEN
ON **ILFORD** COLOUR
FILM

151

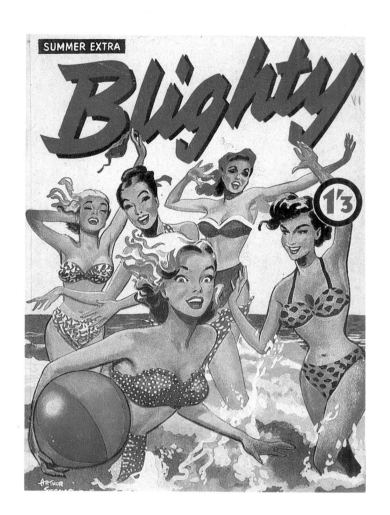

Publishers in any country, in any age have long known the swiftest route to the magazine buyer's wallet, even when inside pages

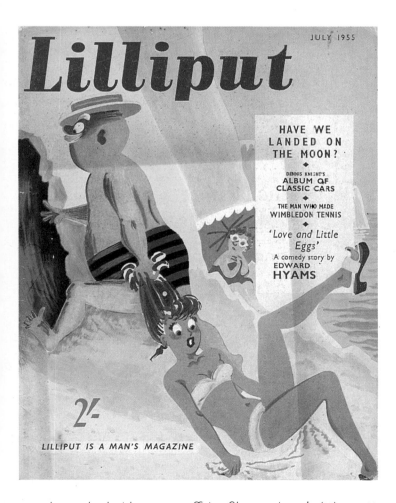

may be packed with current affairs, film gossip or knitting patterns

154 *Cavorting Bluebell Girls fan out along the Cannes seashore, and (right) actress Nicole Maurey welcomes all to the Film Festival, 1961*

Opposite: Austrian
Eva Reuben-Staier
does the rounds
as 1970's Miss World
and gives a cool
smile on a chilly
spring morning on
Bondi Beach, Sydney

Elizabeth Choviski,
Miss Monte Carlo,
grins gamely
despite coming
sixth in Mecca's
Miss World, 1953

What Louis Reard could never have anticipated — the bikini looking androgynous on women who spend more time in the gym than on the beach, hardening soft curves into steely muscles. Left: Miss Bodybuilding, France, 1985. Right: Cory Everson, current title-holder of the prestigious Miss Olympia contest, California, 1985

PICTURE CREDITS

Front cover Popperfoto
Back cover Colorific
US Cover Stern Magazine/Tom Jacobi
2 Stern Magazine/Tom Jacobi
6/7 Photo Source
8/9 Colorific
10 Photo Source (tp), Kobal/Bud Fraker (btm)
11 Sunday Times (tp), Colorific (btm)
12 Kobal Collection
13 BBC Hulton Picture Library
14 Photo Source (tp), Popperfoto (btm)
15 Allan Grant/LIFE © TIME INC 1957
16 John Frost Periodicals
17 Popperfoto (tp), Rex Features Ltd/
   Gunnar Larsen (btm)
18/19 Stern Magazine/Tom Jacobi
20 Liza Bruce/Nicholas Barker
21 Colorific/Claus Meyer
22 Colorific
23 BBC Hulton Picture Library
24 Popperfoto
25-26 Sunday Times
26/27 BBC Hulton Picture Library
28 Norman Parkinson
29 Sunday Times
30/31 Rex Features Ltd
31-32 Rex Features Ltd/Gunnar Larsen
33 Popperfoto
34 Photo Source
35 Sunday Times
36 Transworld Feature Syndicate Ltd
37 Transworld Feature Syndicate Ltd/
   Joe Francki
38-40 Transworld Feature Syndicate Ltd
41 Transworld Feature Syndicate Ltd/
   David Schoen
42-43 Transworld Feature Syndicate Ltd
44/45 Norman Parkinson
46-47 Transworld Feature Syndicate Ltd
48/49 Stern Magazine/Tom Jacobi
50 Frank Spooner Pictures/Gamma
51 Colorific/Rob Lee
52 Popperfoto
53-55 Rex Features Ltd
56 Photo Source
57 Rex Features Ltd
58/59 Sunday Times
60/61 Frank Spooner Pictures/Gamma
62 Rex Features Ltd
62/63 Popperfoto
64 Frank Spooner Pictures/Gamma
65-66 Rex Features Ltd
67 Popperfoto
68 Rex Features Ltd/Jaques Blot
68/69 Rex Features Ltd
69 Photo Source

70/71 Photographers International
72/73 Rex Features Ltd/Gunnar Larsen
74 Misha Erwitt/People Weekly
   © TIME INC 1985
74/75 Rex Features Ltd
75 BBC Hulton Picture Library (tp),
   Syndication International (btm)
76-77 Rex Features Ltd
78 Popperfoto
78/79 Rex Features Ltd
79 Syndication International (tp),
   Popperfoto (btm)
80 American International Pictures
81-83 Kobal Collection
84 Photo Source
84/85 Popperfoto
86-93 Kobal Collection
94/95 BBC Hulton Picture Library
95 Popperfoto
96 Medusa
97 Russ Meyer
98 Kobal Collection
99 Transworld Feature Syndicate Ltd/
   Bruno Bernard
100/101 Rex Features Ltd
102 Rex Features Ltd/Bruno Bernard
103 Transworld Feature Syndicate Ltd
104 Transworld Feature Syndicate Ltd/
   Yoram Kahana
104/105 Kobal Collection
106 Photo Source
107 Terry O'Neill
108 Kobal Collection (tp),
   Scope Photos (btm)
108/109 Kobal Collection
110 Loonus Dean/LIFE © TIME INC
111 Colorific/Aaron Rapoport
112 Colorific
113 Colorific/Claus Meyer
114/115 Image Bank/Jay Maisel
116 Frank Spooner Pictures
117 Co Rentmeester/LIFE © TIME INC
   1970
118/119 Stockphotos
120 Rex Features Ltd
121 Sunday Times
122/123 Georgina Howell
124/125 BBC Hulton Picture Library
126/127 Gamma/Art Seitz
128 BBC Hulton Picture Library
129 The Observer/Peter Keen
130/131 Colorific/Frank Herrmann
132 Syndication International
133 Popperfoto
134 Rex Features Ltd
135-137 Popperfoto
138-140 Transworld Feature Syndicate Ltd
141 Rex Features Ltd

142 Image Bank/Al Satterwhite
143 Image Bank/Derek Berwin
144 Frank Spooner/Chas Gerretsen
145 Stockphotos
146/147 See credit on photo
148 Ford PR
152/153 John Frost Periodicals
154/155 Popperfoto
156 Photo Source
157 BBC Hulton Picture Library
158 Frank Spooner Pictures/A Duclos
159 All-sport/Tony Duffy

Thanks also to the publishers of Stern and
Neue Revue, and to Syndication
International for allowing us to reproduce
magazine covers on pages 149-151 and
152-153.